P9-EMK-596

VIOLENCE AND SOCIETY™

DEADLY SCHOOL AND CAMPUS VIOLENCE

CORONA BREZINA

ROSEN
PUBLISHING®

New York

Published in 2009 by The Rosen Publishing Group, Inc.
29 East 21st Street, New York, NY 10010
www.rosenpublishing.com

Library of Congress Cataloging-in-Publication Data

Brezina, Corona.
Deadly school and campus violence / Corona Brezina.—1st ed.
   p.cm.—(Violence and society)
Includes bibliographical references and index.
ISBN-13: 978-1-4042-1792-8 (library binding)
1. School violence—United States. 2. Campus violence—United States. I. Title.
LB3013.32.B74 2009
371.7'820973—dc22

                                                              2007049695

Manufactured in Malaysia

On the cover: Those affected feel the aftermath of the Virginia Tech school
shootings.

CONTENTS

INTRODUCTION

COUNTDOWN

NBC NEWS

THE KILLER SPEAKS
CHO SEUNG-HUI'S PACKAGE TO NBC

Less than an hour before the massacre, Virginia Tech killer Seung-Hui Cho sent a package of writings, pictures, and a video to NBC News in which he vented his rage and resentment.

The morning of April 16, 2007, opened with tragedy on the campus of Virginia Tech in Blacksburg in southwestern Virginia. At 7:15 AM, a gunman shot and killed two residents of the large dormitory West Ambler Johnston Hall. The shooter vanished from the scene before the police arrived.

Upon arriving at the dormitory, officers from the Virginia Tech Police Department focused their attention on the boyfriend of one of the victims. Even though there was a murderer at large, they decided against canceling classes or locking down the university. The school administration did not notify the community of the shooting until an e-mail was sent out at 9:30 AM. Little did anyone realize that the crisis was only beginning to unfold.

At 9:40 AM, the same gunman opened fire in a classroom in Norris Hall, an engineering building, where an advanced hydrology class was meeting. The police responded to a 911 call five minutes later and found that three of the entrances to the building had been chained shut. Meanwhile, the gunman moved into nearby classrooms, shooting students and teachers. The police finally gained access to the building at 9:51 by shooting the lock out of the door to a machine shop. The gunman shot himself in the head as the police closed in. Thirty-one people, including the gunman, lay dead in Norris Hall. Seventeen others had been injured. It was the deadliest college massacre in United States history.

The attacker was later identified as Seung-Hui Cho, a twenty-three-year-old senior attending Virginia Tech. Cho was born in South Korea, and his family moved to the United States when Cho was eight years old. From the time he was in elementary school, Cho exhibited signs of mental health problems. At Virginia Tech, numerous teachers and students observed disturbing behavior that indicated mental instability. Two female students filed reports with the police complaining of harassment. Nevertheless, Cho was able to buy guns and ammunition in the months before the attack.

In the aftermath of the massacre, the stunned Virginia Tech community began asking how such a tragic event could have occurred in their school. Why did Cho do it? Could the police have taken any further action during the course of the crisis that could have saved lives? Could steps have been taken to avert the massacre? How could a young man with a history of mental illness—documented in police records—have openly purchased handguns?

Across the nation, other communities have also found themselves grappling with such questions in the wake of school attacks. School massacres leave scars on families, schools, and communities that never completely heal. Understanding these past tragedies, however, may help reveal the underlying factors that lead to school massacres and contribute to the prevention of future attacks.

CHAPTER ONE
Schools in Crisis

During the late 1990s, it seemed to many Americans that an epidemic of deadly school violence was sweeping the country. Most of these school shootings occurred in suburbs or small towns, places where residents considered criminal violence an urban problem, not something that could happen in their close-knit communities.

After the horrific Columbine High School shootings in 1999, students seemed to grow more willing to come forward with information about potential school attacks. As a result, a number of plots were foiled. For a time, the epidemic of school shootings seemed to end. Then, in 2005, a student in Minnesota went on a rampage that left ten people dead, including the shooter. The Virginia Tech massacre came two years later, shattering any illusions that school massacres were no longer an issue of concern.

Targeted School Violence

In 1999, the U.S. Secret Service joined the U.S. Department of Education in investigating the pre-attack conditions that led to school shootings. The Secret Service, which is the organization responsible for protecting the president and other public figures, was eminently qualified to assess the factors leading up to school attacks. The study, called the Safe School Initiative, focused on "targeted school violence" in which the attacker specifically chose the school as the site of the attack and

attended—or had attended—the school itself. This excluded instances of violence such as gang shootings or random attacks.

The Safe School Initiative examined a number of incidents of school violence dating back to 1974. The goal was to determine whether school attacks could be anticipated and prevented. Researchers tracked trends of behaviors and other warning signs that had been observed in past attacks, with the intent of using

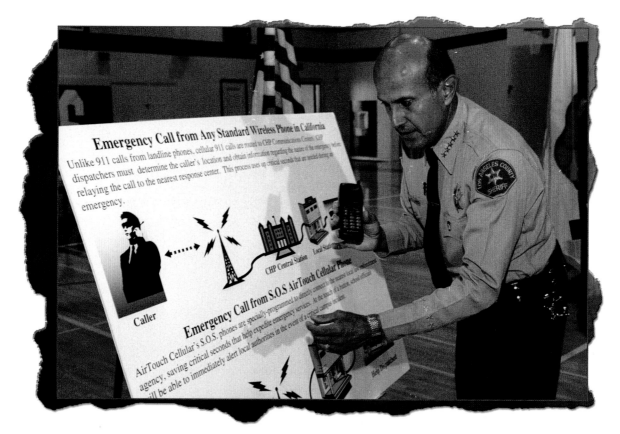

After a rash of high-profile school shootings during the 1990s, many schools adopted new security measures to deal with potential attacks.

this information to recommend strategies for preventing future violence.

There is no simple way to explain or avert school attacks. Attackers come from a variety of backgrounds. They attack for many different reasons. There is no single factor that indicates a likelihood that a student will turn into a killer. It is a combination of causes, ranging from psychological issues to relationships with peers to a lack of detection among adults, that can lead to school massacres.

Justice for the Young

What is the appropriate sentence for school killers who turn a gun on their fellow students? Many Americans believe that they deserve the death penalty, or at least life imprisonment. The opposing view is that children deserve greater leniency than adults, since they are too young to fully understand the consequences of their actions. In 2005, the U.S. Supreme Court issued a ruling that banned the execution of murderers who had been under eighteen when they committed a crime that would be punishable by the death sentence for adults. The justices cited the Eight Amendment of the Constitution, which prohibits cruel and unusual punishment.

In most cases, adolescent school shooters can be tried in court as adults. They are likely to receive a sentence of life in prison without possibility of parole. Most other countries of the world are more lenient on young offenders. The United Nations Convention on the Rights of the Child specifically prohibits sentencing juveniles to life imprisonment without opportunity for parole. Out of nearly two hundred member nations of the UN, only the United States and Somalia have not ratified the accord.

In 2005, the Supreme Court took up the case of Christopher Simmons, who had killed a woman at age seventeen, and ruled the death penalty unconstitutional for juvenile offenders.

High-Profile Tragedy

School massacres seize the attention of the public. In 1970, members of the National Guard opened fire on a crowd of students at Kent State, in Ohio, who were protesting the Vietnam War. Four protesters were killed and ten others were wounded. The shootings horrified the nation.

The cluster of school attacks in the late 1990s left parents and students in a state of fear. Every day, newspapers and news broadcasts covered yet another angle on the school shootings crisis. Some have speculated that the intense media coverage and public fascination with these incidents actually helped fuel subsequent "copycat" attacks. The real risk of fatal school violence, however, was statistically very low. According to the Safe School

The Kent State shootings on May 4, 1970, left four students dead and served to intensify the opposition of the youth movement to the Vietnam War.

Initiative, a child had less than a one in one million chance of dying in school as a result of suicide or homicide. Students were far more likely to be involved in lesser forms of violence or crime, such as theft or fighting. In addition, young people were much likelier to be the victims of homicide or other crimes outside of school.

Even when school attackers targeted specific individuals, in over half of the cases, the targets were teachers, principals, or other adults. Among nontargeted victims, adults made up over one-third of those who were killed or injured.

The damage done by school massacres, however, goes beyond a tally of the dead and wounded. The incidents leave witnesses—particularly children—to cope with post-traumatic stress for years afterward. Schools are transformed into crime scenes, and memories of the tragedy haunt the community. Nationally, incidents of school violence make Americans wonder whether the United States can truly provide secure schools for its children.

CHAPTER TWO
Inside a School Shooting

On April 20, 1999, Columbine High School in Colorado became the scene of the deadliest high school shooting in United States history up to that time. Seventeen days before they were due to graduate, eighteen-year-old Eric Harris and seventeen-year-old Dylan Klebold stormed their school, killing twelve students and a teacher, and wounding twenty-two others. They committed suicide at the end of their rampage. The Columbine massacre stunned and horrified the American people. It was the nation's deadliest mass killing in the period between the Oklahoma City bombing of 1995 and the terrorist attacks on September 11, 2001.

The Columbine Massacre

On the day of the attack, Harris and Klebold arrived at Columbine High School around 11:00 in the morning. Each carried a duffel bag containing a propane bomb, which they placed in the cafeteria. The bombs were set to detonate at 11:17 AM, when hundreds of students would be eating lunch. Harris and Klebold anticipated that the powerful explosion would cause massive destruction in the cafeteria and send a panicked crowd fleeing the school. The attackers sat in their cars—also rigged with bombs—and waited for the detonation. They planned to shoot at students as they fled into the parking lot. Between them, they carried a 9 mm

In the aftermath of the Columbine massacre, family and friends rallied together to cope with the tragedy that had struck their community.

carbine rifle, a semiautomatic handgun, two sawed-off shotguns, and an array of bombs, ammunition, and knives.

The bombs planted in the cafeteria failed to explode due to faulty detonators. Harris and Klebold, both wearing black trench coats, decided to storm the school. They headed toward the west entrance of the building. The massacre began when they gunned down two students eating lunch nearby on the lawn. They also shot at several other students in the area. Harris continued to

target students outside while Klebold briefly entered the cafeteria, perhaps to see why the bombs hadn't exploded. After he rejoined Harris, they threw several pipe bombs around the area.

Word of the assault spread, and people inside the school could hear the sounds of shots and explosions. Patti Nielson—a teacher on hall duty—and a student standing nearby were injured by glass and debris as Klebold and Harris shot out the glass

Eric Harris and Dylan Klebold, wearing their trench coats, walk through the hallway at Columbine High School in a video they made for a school project.

doorway. The two victims retreated into the library, and Nielson called the police. By this time, the police were receiving a flurry of 911 calls. Harris fired at a sheriff's deputy arriving on the scene. The deputy returned fire, missing. Both boys ran through the shattered doors into the school, shooting at panicked teachers and students.

Harris again exchanged gunfire with the police before joining Klebold, and the pair roamed the halls throwing bombs and shooting at anyone they encountered. Victims and witnesses would later state that the attackers were smiling and laughing as they went on their rampage. One victim was science teacher Dave Sanders, who had helped evacuate the cafeteria before heading upstairs. He crawled into a nearby classroom and died despite students' attempts to save his life, the only teacher killed in the massacre.

Harris and Klebold next entered the library. Due to upcoming exams, over fifty students were studying there during the lunch period. The shooters yelled for all of the "jocks" to stand up. When nobody obeyed, Harris announced that he would "just start shooting." The first victim was a mentally retarded student, according to some reports the only person in the room who had not tried to hide.

As they stalked through the library, randomly shooting at terrified students huddled under tables and desks, Harris and Klebold taunted their victims and laughed at the agony and devastation they were causing. Harris said, "Peek-a-boo," to a girl hiding under a table before shooting her. Another wounded girl cried out, "Oh, my God!" Klebold asked her, "Do you believe in God?" She replied, "Yes." "Why?" Klebold said. He walked away without shooting her. Klebold also spared a friend who had been

studying in the library. Harris and Klebold sporadically shot out the library window at officers and students being evacuated from the school, threw explosives, and took aim at computers and other random objects. Within the space of about eight minutes, the two gunmen killed ten students in the library. When a girl asked why they were doing it, Harris answered, "This is payback."

The pair left the library and walked through the halls, randomly firing their weapons and throwing explosives. Although they could see students barricaded in classrooms, they did not try to target any more victims. After a few minutes, they made their way to the cafeteria. Footage from a security camera shows that they made an unsuccessful attempt to detonate one of the propane bombs in the duffel bag and sipped some water abandoned on a table. Shortly afterward, Harris and Klebold returned to the library and took their own lives.

Eric Harris and Dylan Klebold

Why did they do it? Experts have considered a variety of possible factors: bullying and other pressures at school, mental illness, obsession with and easy access to guns and weapons, violence in entertainment media, racism and religious intolerance, and the "goth" subculture. There is still no absolute consensus on which forces were key to pushing them toward committing a horrific massacre.

In many ways, Eric Harris and Dylan Klebold appeared to be normal teenagers. They lived in a quiet community in suburban Denver, and both came from stable, middle-class families. Many people found Harris personable and bright. Klebold was shy

A senior group picture of Columbine High School Class of 1999 shows Eric Harris and Dylan Klebold in the back row.

Wanting to Be Famous

Eric Harris and Dylan Klebold did not plan a mere school shooting; they intended their attack on Columbine to rival the destruction of the Oklahoma City bombing. At school, they were on the fringes of the social order. After their deaths, though, their names would be notorious around the world. They speculated on who might make a movie about the attack, with Quentin Tarantino being their first choice. In his writings, Harris mused on whether authors would write books about him.

Harris and Klebold were not the only school attackers who were excited about the celebrity that would follow their attack. Many school shooters eagerly anticipated that their names would be in headlines and on TV news. In 1994, for example, seventeen-year-old Clay Shrout murdered his parents and younger sisters at home. He then proceeded to Larry A. Ryle High School in Union, Kentucky, where he held a class hostage at gunpoint for a half hour before surrendering without further bloodshed. As he was preparing to leave for school, Shrout had encountered a neighbor and told him that he was going to be on CNN.

and his teachers described him as a slacker, yet he had made plans to attend college after graduation. A few days before the massacre, he attended his senior prom with Robyn Anderson, a friend, and talked optimistically about the future.

After the massacre, however, investigators pieced together a far more disturbing portrayal of the killers. Harris and Klebold

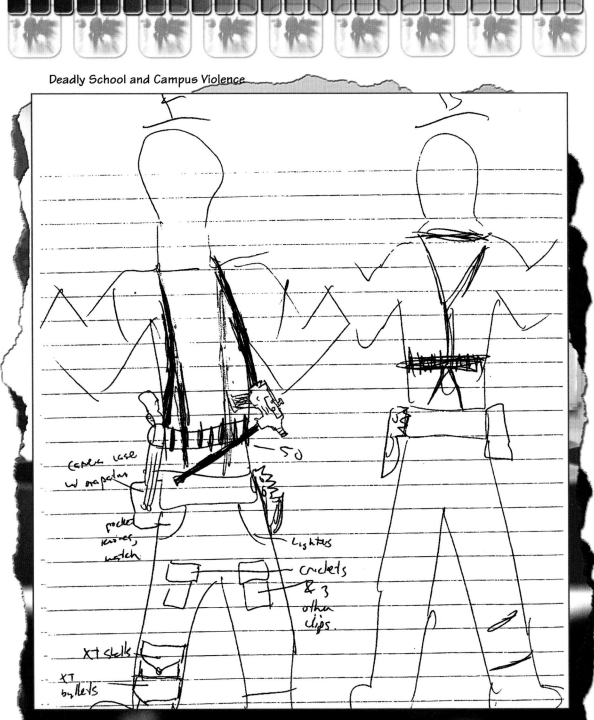

In 2006, the Jefferson County Sheriff's Office released hundreds of pages of documents pertaining to the Columbine massacre, including this sketch drawn by Dylan Klebold.

left behind violent and hate-filled writings and videos. They built bombs, acquired an arsenal of weapons, and vandalized neighbors' homes, boasting publicly about these incidents on online "mission logs." Harris once showed off a homemade bomb at the pizza restaurant where both boys worked.

After being arrested for breaking into a van, Harris and Klebold both had to participate in counseling and community service. The parents of a friend, Brooks Brown, filed a complaint against Harris after discovering threats against Brooks he had posted on a Web site. Klebold wrote a story for an English class in which a killer stalks his victims. It so disturbed his teacher that she reported it to a guidance counselor and Klebold's parents.

Harris was fascinated with Nazism, and Klebold followed his lead despite being half Jewish. The date of the massacre, April 20, was the birthday of Adolf Hitler. On that day, Harris wore a T-shirt reading "Natural Selection." Klebold's read "Wrath."

CHAPTER THREE
Characteristics of Attackers

Could Harris and Klebold's plan at Columbine have been anticipated? Could the massacre have been prevented? The Safe School Initiative, released in 2002 by the Secret Service and the Department of Education, examined the Columbine attack as well as thirty-six other incidents in order to analyze common characteristics, knowledge that could contribute to future prevention efforts. They drew up ten key findings from their research. Many of these findings fit the circumstances of the Columbine massacre.

The study found that "there is no accurate or useful 'profile' of students who engaged in targeted school violence." Attackers came from a variety of different circumstances. Some were loners, but others seemed to fit in socially at school. They also differed in terms of their performance at school. For the most part, they received average or above-average grades. In general, there was no specific change in their lives—such as issues with friends or disciplinary problems—prior to the attack that directly spurred their actions. There was also no clear pattern of race, family situation, or economic background.

The report warned against identifying students as possible threats based on how they might resemble the same "type" as a prior school shooter. For example, attention turned to the goth youth subculture, which often includes wearing black clothing, including the long trench coats that Harris and Klebold wore. The pair enjoyed violent video games, violent

Following the rash of school shootings in the 1990s, schools and the media focused attention on fringe groups such as the "goth" subculture among young adults.

movies, and music with violent lyrics. Nevertheless, the overwhelming majority of students with similar interests do not pose a possible attack risk. The Safe School Initiative emphasized that tracking behavioral patterns, rather than profiling, could prove an effective means of preventing future attacks.

Another finding was that many attackers felt bullied, persecuted, or injured by others prior to the attack. School

attackers often felt that they had been the target of harassment and teasing, and this was a factor in their resolve to retaliate. After the Columbine massacre, Columbine High School came under scrutiny for tolerance of bullying. Athletics were highly emphasized at Columbine High School. The social order was dominated by jocks, some of whom had a reputation for frequent bullying and taunting of students they disliked. Many of the students in the middle of Columbine's social order followed the jocks' example in ostracizing certain students, or kicking them out of their social circles. As a result, some students felt like outcasts from the main student body.

Some experts have countered that Harris and Klebold were not truly outcasts from the entire student body. They had a circle of friends that they hung out with, and they participated in extracurricular activities. Nevertheless, both boys wrote in their journals about not fitting in at school and feeling like outcasts.

A video shot by Klebold in the school hallways documents one instance: as Klebold and Harris pass by a group of athletes, two members knock him off balance and laugh as they walk away. Apparently, such harassment was routine. Certain students were regularly tripped, pelted with food, and thrown into lockers. Harassers would taunt their victims, especially with homophobic slurs that cast doubt on their masculinity. Once, when students in a car threw a bottle at them, Klebold told Brooks Brown that it was a frequent occurrence.

According to the Safe School Initiative, about 75 percent of the attackers in the study experienced such bullying prior to their attack. In a 1987 incident in DeKalb, Missouri, twelve-year-old Nathan D. Faris endured insults about his weight and bookish tendencies until one Friday when he threatened to bring a gun to school on Monday. He carried through with it, only to

Characteristics of Attackers

have his weapon laughed at by his schoolmates, who taunted it as a "toy" gun. Faris proved that his pistol was authentic by killing a classmate and then shooting himself.

Eighteen years after Faris brought a gun to school, and six years after Columbine, sixteen-year-old Jeff Weise went on a rampage on the Red Lake Chippewa Indian Reservation in Minnesota. On March 21, 2005, he killed his grandfather and his companion at home, then drove to the Red Lake High School. There, he killed a security guard, a teacher, and five students before turning his gun on himself. In the year before the massacre, Weise had reported teasing and harassment from his peers.

Before his 2005 Minnesota rampage, Jeff Weise had a history of behavioral problems and expressed admiration for Hitler. He used the alias "NativeNazi" on the Internet.

Coping with Loss and Failure

The Safe School Initiative found that many of the attackers had been severely depressed prior to the attack. A number of possible factors contributed to their desperation, such as a crisis in a romantic relationship, the death or illness of a friend or relative, or a punishment for wrongdoing. Many had expressed suicidal thoughts or made suicide attempts. Some of the attackers, like Harris and Klebold, ended their rampage with suicide or anticipated that they would not survive the incident.

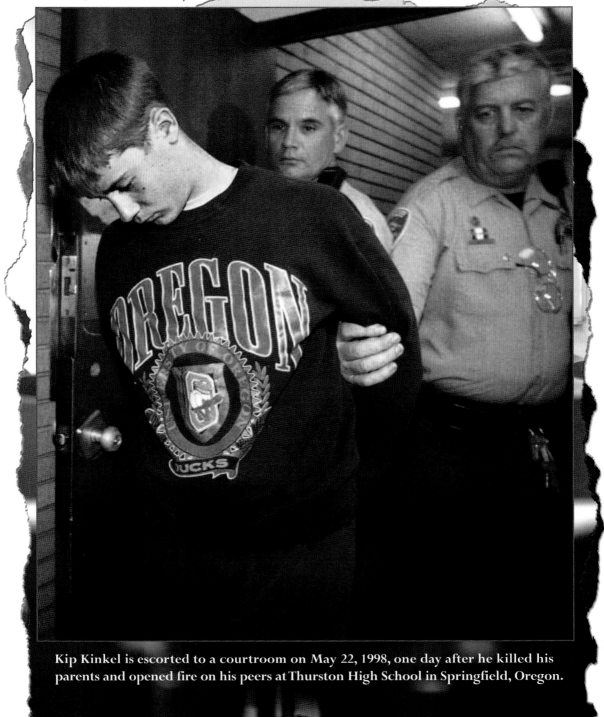

Kip Kinkel is escorted to a courtroom on May 22, 1998, one day after he killed his parents and opened fire on his peers at Thurston High School in Springfield, Oregon.

Klebold's journal reveals depression, anger, and broodings on suicide. On April 19, 1999, he wrote about preparing for the attack the next day: "What fun is life without a little death? It's interesting, when I'm in my human form, knowing I'm going to die." Harris, as well, reported feeling depression, loneliness, and homicidal and suicidal thoughts in a form that he filled out for a therapist a year before the Columbine massacre. Jeff Weise also had a history of suicidal tendencies. He cut his wrists in 2004 and was put on Prozac, an antidepressant.

On May 20, 1998, fifteen-year-old Kipland Kinkel shot and killed his parents in their Springfield, Oregon, home. The next morning, he took three guns and two knives to school with him concealed under a long trench coat, as well as a bag full of ammunition. Kinkel entered the crowded school cafeteria and opened fire, killing two students before being overpowered and disarmed. As Kinkel was pinned down, he kept screaming that he wanted to die and begged to be shot. When the police later searched him, they found two bullets taped to his chest. Kinkel explained that he'd wanted extra bullets in order to kill himself in case he ran out of ammunition—despite the fact that he carried enough ammunition to kill over one thousand people.

The Safe School Initiative did not find that mental illness was prevalent among attackers, but only about a third of the subjects had undergone a mental health evaluation before the incident. Other studies have estimated that rates of serious mental illness might actually be much higher. It is very rare, however, for a school shooter to successfully plead an insanity defense in court.

After the Columbine massacre, Eric Harris's psychiatric state came under scrutiny. A team of FBI psychiatrists diagnosed him as a psychopath, a psychiatric condition characterized by hostility

and lack of empathy. Many of Harris's notebook rants start with "DO YOU KNOW WHAT I HATE!!!?" They express his contempt for his peers, as well as for "stupid" people, country music, homosexuals, wrestling fans, slow drivers, *Star Wars* fans, and much more. Harris also reveled in deceiving people. After being sentenced for breaking into the van, he was discharged early from his community service program for good behavior. His parole officer wrote that Harris was likely to do well in life. On his Web site, Harris gloated at fooling everybody. Some have questioned the diagnosis of psychopathy, though, since Harris also had a volatile temper and did not completely match the criteria for the disorder.

Kip Kinkel exhibited many symptoms of possible mental illness as well. He claimed to hear auditory hallucinations—voices in his head—telling him to kill. He also appeared paranoid and delusional, believing, for example, that the "Disney dollar" was set to become America's main form of currency. Since mental illness is inherited, Kinkel's lawyers studied his family history. They found that numerous relatives on both sides of his family had been diagnosed with serious mental illnesses such as schizophrenia or bipolar disorder, and many had been confined to mental institutions.

Causes for Concern

The Safe School Initiative noted that in more than 90 percent of the attacks, some aspect of the attacker's behavior had caused alarm in school officials, parents, teachers, police, or other students. In some cases, the behavior had been directly linked to the subsequent attack, such as threats or possessions of weapons. Other warning signs were more general, such as a cruelty to

Desperate to make friends, Michael Carneal thought that he would impress other students by opening fire on his classmates at Heath High School in Kentucky.

animals or an extreme obsession with violence. Harris's and Klebold's attitudes, writings, and interest in weapons caused concern in a number of others—their parents, teachers, the police, and other students, as well as Brooks Brown's parents— but authorities did not piece together the pattern of behaviors until after the massacre.

Hindsight often reveals a clear picture of alarming signs leading up to an attack. In 1997, fourteen-year-old Michael Carneal brought a number of rifles, a pistol, and nearly one thousand rounds of ammunition to Heath High School in West Paducah, Kentucky. He showed off his weapons to his friends and put earplugs in his ears. Then Carneal opened fire on a circle of students gathered together to pray. Three students were killed.

Carneal had exhibited a number of disturbing behaviors before the incident. He turned in violent writings for English class, including one in which he tortured and killed classmates. Carneal had stolen guns, CDs, and other items and taken them to school to impress his friends. He obtained a copy of a book on making bombs. Like Kinkel, he was disarmed and pleaded to be shot after the massacre ended.

Premeditated Acts

Most of the attackers examined for the Safe School Initiative put thought into their attack before the event; they did not just spontaneously snap. More than half of the attackers had conceived of the idea over a month in advance. Nearly all of the attackers planned a strategy of attack and made preparations, such as obtaining weapons or choosing the time and location.

Notes that Harris and Klebold wrote in each other's yearbooks indicate that they had the idea for the massacre at least a

Students at Westside Middle School in Arkansas huddle in shock after an attack by Mitchell Johnson and Andrew Golden left four students and a teacher dead.

year in advance. They plotted the attack like a military operation. They carefully considered the timing and different possible locations, aiming for the greatest possible destruction, and tested weapons beforehand. If their homemade propane bombs had erupted, the explosion could have killed hundreds of people. The pair even set off bombs in a field some distance away from school beforehand as a distraction for the authorities.

In 1998, at Westside Middle School in Jonesboro, Arkansas, Mitchell Johnson and Andrew Golden devised a cold-blooded and deadly plan. Johnson stole the keys to his stepfather's van one March morning, and the boys loaded the vehicle with firearms. Both wore camouflage. They made their way to a wooded hillside overlooking the playground. Golden ran to the school, pulled the fire alarm, and ran back. Students and teachers evacuating the building walked directly into the line of fire. The shooters killed five people before fleeing into the woods. The police caught them before they could reach the van, where they had packed supplies and a map of their escape route. At the time, Mitchell Johnson was thirteen years old. Andrew Golden was eleven. Both were eventually released from detention when they turned twenty-one.

Involvement of Other Students

In the aftermath of a school massacre, authorities often found that other people had known some details of the attack beforehand and did not sound the alarm, despite the potential disastrous consequences. Attackers would make vague threats, boast about their violent plans, warn people about "something big" or an upcoming "day of reckoning," or even share their entire plot with

a friend. In most cases, these were peers or siblings—adults rarely had prior knowledge. They would often say later that they did not think the threat was real, that they thought the attacker was joking, or that they were too afraid of the attacker to snitch.

Harris's and Klebold's resentment and violent tirades were known among their friends. Harris talked of killing people and even about blowing up the school, but people did not believe that his intentions were serious. Neither Harris nor Klebold shared any specific details of their plan immediately prior to the massacre. On the morning of the attack, however, they encountered Brooks Brown in the school parking lot. Harris warned him to leave immediately. Brown went on his way without realizing what Harris and Klebold were planning. When he heard gunfire later on, he called the police.

The Safe School Initiative stated that fewer than one in six attackers threatened their targets beforehand. The report also stated that the target could be an individual, a group, or, as in the Columbine attack, the school itself. Harris and Klebold had written a "hit list" containing dozens of names—largely consisting of boys who bullied them and girls who rejected them—but they did not target specific individuals during the massacre.

In a 1997 incident in Bethel, Alaska, the attacker broadcast his intentions far more publicly in advance of his attack. Friends encouraged sixteen-year-old Evan Ramsey to take a stand against the students who bullied and taunted him. One friend showed him how to use a shotgun. Another planned to take pictures. On the morning of February 19, a crowd on a balcony waited for Ramsey to make an entrance below. They knew that Ramsey had something planned—he had told some of his friends that he was going to bring a gun to school to shoot the principal of the

Bethel Regional School. When he arrived, Ramsey shot and killed a star basketball player and then the principal, both within view of the balcony.

Access to Weapons

The phrase "school massacre" is often used interchangeably with "school shooting," although some attackers carried other weapons such as knives or bombs as well. Two-thirds of the attackers examined in the Safe School Initiative were known to have used weapons in the past. Half had used a gun. When they mounted their attack, over two-thirds used firearms found in their home or belonging to a relative.

Harris and Klebold spent months obtaining weapons in advance of the Columbine massacre. Their friend Robyn Anderson, who was eighteen years old, bought them two shotguns and a rifle at a gun show. At the time, both boys were underage and could not legally purchase firearms themselves. They bought their handgun from an acquaintance and spent hundreds of dollars on propane tanks and other bomb-making supplies. No adults expressed concern over their activities, even when a gun shop owner called Harris's house with the message that the ammunition order was ready for pickup. Eric Harris's father answered the phone. He replied that he had not ordered ammunition and did not follow up on the matter.

Other attackers had an even easier time assembling their arsenals. Jeff Weise used a shotgun and two handguns belonging to his grandfather. Michael Carneal stole a pistol and two shotguns from his father and stole five other rifles from a friend's home.

Kipland Kinkel had long been fascinated with weapons. His parents bought guns for him in an attempt to appease their

troublemaking son. Kinkel obtained books on making bombs and once gave a class presentation on making bombs out of household chemicals. His mother unknowingly supplied him with some of his bomb-making materials, believing that they were for a science project. When the police inventoried Kinkel's weapons collection after his attack, they found nearly fifty knives, seven guns, and a number of homemade bombs.

HARRIS
VEHICLE

The weapons and supplies taken from Eric Harris's car after the Columbine massacre were only a small part of the arsenal that Harris and Klebold assembled in preparation for the attack.

Young Andrew Golden had won awards for his marksmanship from the age of nine. On the morning of their attack, Golden and Mitchell Johnson stole three pistols from Golden's father. They determined that the guns were not suitable for long-range shooting, however. The boys then broke into Golden's grandparents' house and stole four more handguns and three rifles.

In most cases studied for the Safe School Initiative, the attacker surrendered, left the scene, or was overpowered without law enforcement intervention. Only about a quarter of the cases were stopped by the police or other law enforcement personnel. Half of the incidents ended in fewer than fifteen minutes.

CHAPTER FOUR
Other Attacks

O n October 28, 2002, Robert Flores stormed his school armed with five handguns. He killed three teachers before shooting himself. Afterward, fellow students and teachers stated that Flores had been doing poorly in his studies and was depressed about his personal circumstances. He had also talked about suicide and made threats against the school. Flores's school was the University of Arizona, and his victims were all professors in the College of Nursing. He was forty-one years old when he went on his rampage.

Some of the most horrendous school massacres have been committed by adults. The common perception of a mass murderer is of a disturbed individual who suddenly snaps and starts shooting random strangers, but in reality, that scenario is rare. A majority of mass murders are planned in advance, and the targets are family members or acquaintances. The most common motive is revenge for perceived injustices. Other possible driving factors include profit, sheer hatred, or a grievance against the "system." Some possible motives of adult mass murderers are similar to those of young adult attackers. While young adults often claim that bullying or teasing compelled them to attack, adult killers tend to report that they had received unfair treatment or harassment at work.

There is one key difference between adult attackers and young attackers: young attackers are more likely to involve their peers in their plot. They might brag about the

impending attack. Other students may help them in their preparations, often without knowing their plans. Adult mass murderers, on the other hand, generally do not share their plans with others or broadcast their intentions.

College Massacres

In analyzing college-age attackers, should they be put in the same category as young adult attackers or should they be grouped with adult mass murderers? College students are still in the process of making the transition to adulthood. Their social structure generally still revolves around school life. To some extent, they are still under the supervision of their elders, such as teachers, counselors, academic advisers, and dorm coordinators. On the other hand, college students may have had life experiences that gave them motivations and means beyond those of younger attackers.

One of the most horrific mass murders in United States history was committed by twenty-five-year-old Charles Whitman in 1966 on the campus of the University of Texas. Whitman had joined the Marine Corps after graduating high school, and he achieved the class of sharpshooter. After an honorable discharge, Whitman enrolled in the University of Texas. Although he appeared to be an upstanding citizen, Whitman had a dark side.

He had been demoted for minor offenses during his stint in the Marine Corps, and his family and friends feared his explosive temper. In the spring of 1966, Whitman began to find the pressures of his life overwhelming. On July 31, he killed his wife and mother. The next morning, he took up position at the top of the three-hundred-foot-high (ninety-one-meter-high) clock tower that overlooked the campus. Heavily armed with an assortment

A puff of smoke wafts from Charles Whitman's gun during his 1966 sniper attack from the clock tower at the University of Texas.

of firearms, he barricaded himself inside and began targeting random passersby. Whitman killed fourteen people before being surrounded and fatally shot by police.

Seung-Hui Cho, the Virginia Tech shooter, was withdrawn and uncommunicative from a young age. Cho may have experienced bullying during his early years, but he never discussed it.

The Bath School Massacre

In some cases, a school attacker targets the institution itself, not specific victims. This was the case in the little-known Bath, Michigan, school massacre of 1927. Andrew Kehoe blamed the newly constructed Bath Consolidated School for his troubles. In his mind, the high taxes that paid for the school caused him to lose his farm.

Hired as a school maintenance man, Kehoe rigged the building with explosives over a period of many months. On May 18, the last day of school, Kehoe murdered his wife and blew up many of the buildings on his farm. He then proceeded to the school and detonated the explosives planted inside. Half of the building collapsed, leaving dozens of people trapped underneath the rubble.

A half hour later, Kehoe drove up and called the school superintendent over to his truck. Kehoe then detonated a load of dynamite in the vehicle with a rifle shot. The explosion killed both men as well as three bystanders. In total, forty-five people died in the disaster, including thirty-eight children. The Bath School massacre was the deadliest mass killing in the United States until the Oklahoma City bombing of 1995.

He first exhibited homicidal and suicidal thoughts shortly after Columbine, when he turned in an English paper that greatly alarmed his teacher. As a result, he underwent a psychological evaluation and was prescribed an antidepressant. Cho's mental health condition worsened during his last couple of years of college, and he became totally alienated from his peers. In a videotape he sent to NBC shortly before his attack, he ranted hatefully about other students and vowed revenge.

School Invasions

School attackers are not always students at the institution they target; adults occasionally invade and assault schools with tragic results. The motives of these attackers vary widely. They may hold a grudge against the school for personal reasons. They may choose to attack a school in order to draw attention to themselves, anticipating that the incident will generate shock, outrage, and considerable media coverage.

On October 2, 2006, Charles Roberts entered a one-room Amish schoolhouse in the small town of Nickel Mines, Pennsylvania. He held ten young girls in the class hostage and barricaded the door. Eventually, Roberts shot and killed five girls, left five others injured, and killed himself. Afterward, police found no indication that the thirty-two-year-old milk truck driver held any particular resentment against the Amish community or the school itself.

Internationally, some of the deadliest school massacres in recent years were committed by adult invaders. In 1989, twenty-five-year-old Marc Lépine quietly entered a crowded classroom at the University of Montreal School of Engineering in Canada, a school that had refused to admit him. He pulled

This Amish one-room schoolhouse in Nickel Mines, Pennsylvania, became a crime scene after Charles Roberts's 2006 attack left five girls dead. The building has since been demolished.

out a semiautomatic rifle and ordered all of the men in the room to leave. Lépine shot and killed nine women, then continued his rampage in the hallway, killing five more women, before shooting himself. In a suicide note, he ranted about "feminists" who had ruined his life. In 1996, a forty-three-year-old former scoutmaster in Scotland named Thomas Hamilton resolved to take revenge after he was dismissed for improper conduct. Armed with four

handguns, he opened fire on a kindergarten, killing sixteen young children and a teacher before committing suicide. In 2002, in Erfurt, Germany, nineteen-year-old Robert Steinhäuser stormed his former school, targeting the teachers he blamed for his expulsion. He killed sixteen people—including thirteen teachers—before turning his gun on himself.

In 2002, Robert Steinhäuser went on a deadly rampage at Gutenberg Gymnasium (high school) in Erfurt, Germany, going from room to room targeting teachers.

These adult mass murderers gave no warning before targeting a classroom. In some cases, they had no personal connection to their victims. Unlike adult killers, however, young adults often signal their intentions in advance. If educators and students recognize warning signs before the event, school attacks planned by students can be prevented and tragedy can be averted.

CHAPTER FIVE

Averting School Massacres

For every instance of a school attack that briefly dominates media headlines, there are numerous foiled plots that do not receive as much coverage. In 2001, a handful of students in New Bedford, Massachusetts, began planning an attack on New Bedford High School that would rival Columbine in destruction. The plot came to the attention of the police when one member of the group—the only girl involved—warned a former teacher. A police raid turned up weapons, bomb-making instructions, and Nazi literature in the ringleader's house. Five students ranging in age from fifteen to seventeen were arrested and charged with conspiracy to commit murder.

College massacres have also been prevented. Earlier in 2001, nineteen-year-old Al DeGuzman, a student at De Anza Community College in California, had film developed at a local drugstore. A young woman who worked in the photo lab was disturbed by the pictures, which showed DeGuzman posing amidst firearms and explosives. Police searched his home and found an arsenal of weapons. DeGuzman, who was obsessed with the Columbine massacre, had been preparing for a massive attack on the cafeteria of his school.

Intervention Efforts

One of the goals of the Safe School Initiative was to provide guidance on investigating and intervening in potential school

Kelly Bennet, who worked at a photo counter in Cupertino, California, notified police about Al DeGuzman's suspicious photographs. They arrested him just hours before he planned to launch his attack.

attacks. The report emphasizes the importance of detecting behavior and communications that might indicate that a student poses a threat. If investigators receive a piece of information on a possible threat, they should tactfully determine whether there have been related causes of concern.

School attackers do not suddenly "snap." They gradually build up to a resolution to mount an attack, sometimes leaving

Gender Roles

On January 29, 1979, sixteen-year-old Brenda Spencer opened fire on a crowd of students and employees at Cleveland Elementary School in San Diego, California. The principal and a custodian were killed. Spencer used a rifle she had received as a Christmas gift from her father. When questioned about her motives, she said, "I just don't like Mondays . . . I just did it because it's a way to cheer the day up." Years after the attack, she stated that she had hoped that the police would kill her in the aftermath.

Spencer's rampage broke with one of the trends observed in the Safe School Initiative: every one of the attackers the researchers analyzed was male. They did not speculate on the reasons behind this finding. (Spencer did not fit the criteria of the study because she never attended the school she attacked.) Other studies have indicated that in addition to being unlikely to mount an attack, girls are far more likely than boys to tip off authorities about a planned massacre.

signals that can be assembled into a pattern. Has the student made threats, boasts, or warnings? Could his friends have encouraged plans for violence? Do his records indicate any past misbehavior or other troubling incidents? Does he show signs of depression or difficulty with personal problems? Is he singled out for bullying or teasing? Does he have access to firearms? In order to investigate a potential threat as quickly as possible, there must be clear lines of communication between teachers, parents, law enforcement personnel, and the other adults involved in the case.

In order for students to play an active role in preventing school violence, administrators and teachers must create a school climate in which students feel comfortable reporting potential threats. Discipline should be applied consistently for all students. If students misbehave, they must receive appropriate discipline whether they're star athletes or slackers. Teachers and counselors should not tolerate bullying. When a student does report threats or disturbing behaviors, the student's identity should be kept confidential and there should be a system in place for following up on the information.

Adolescence is a time when children begin to test their independence and assert themselves as individuals. Teens show a different side of their personalities to their peers than to their parents, teachers, and other adults. In the aftermath of a school attack, adults often said that they never saw the troubled side of the attacker. It often came out that fellow students, who may have witnessed more warning signs, were reluctant to notify an adult. Many were afraid of being labeled a "snitch" by their peers if they reported a threat they did not consider serious. After Columbine, more students seemed to be willing to come forward and inform adults of suspicious behavior. Often, these reported

Wisconsin governor Jim Doyle talks about his state budget proposal, which includes a hike in educational funding that would limit class sizes in schools.

threats were indeed baseless. In a number of cases, however, the authorities uncovered plots against the school and averted potentially deadly attacks.

The Debate on Keeping Schools Safe

Schools should be secure environments that promote learning; parents, teachers, counselors, school administrators, law enforcement officials, and students all agree on that much. There is less agreement on the appropriate steps to ensure this.

Many schools have improved security by implementing physical measures such as security cameras, metal detectors, fences, and security-minded design in building new facilities. Critics claim that these measures are very expensive and offer a false sense of security. For one thing, resourceful students can circumvent such measures. For another, schools might be tempted to rely on these measures and neglect other efforts such as crisis preparedness, antibullying programs, and self-assessment within the school's administration. Teachers and students in high-security schools often complain that metal detectors and other physical measures turn the school into a hostile environment.

Schools have also increased security by instituting "zero tolerance" policies in which harsh punishments are mandatory for certain offenses, such as weapons violence. A student who brings a gun to school, for example, would automatically be expelled for a year. Critics say that administrators should take the circumstances of the offense into account. They cite many instances of injustice resulting from zero tolerance policies, such as a third-grade child being suspended for having a tiny

Concerns over school violence have led to increased security measures in schools. Students at Curie High School in Chicago are required to wear ID cards at all times.

plastic gun on a key chain. In addition, critics claim that zero tolerance policies cause a further barrier between teens and adults, hampering free communication that is so important to averting school attacks.

Some experts have called for increased mental health services in schools. Teachers could refer troubled students to a counselor or social worker. These health care professionals

could help students deal with issues such as depression, and they would also be in a position to pass on warnings about potential threats. Critics point out that increased access to mental health services would be expensive and that there is no certainty that counselors or social workers would be able to detect and deter school attackers.

Any potential gun buyer in Colorado must pass a background check. In the wake of incidents such as Columbine and the Virginia Tech massacre, new laws regulating gun sales have been enacted.

One of the most controversial aspects of reducing school violence—as well as overall weapons violence in the United States—is gun control. Every recent school massacre has involved guns, and many young school shooters were easily able to gain access to them. Gun control activists champion various restrictions on these lethal weapons, such as stricter background checks for gun buyers, required safety locks on some guns, or banning outright some of the most dangerous weapons. Many gun owners, on the other hand, point out that the Constitution provides for citizens' rights to bear arms and that making it more difficult for law-abiding people to buy weapons will not help keep them out of the hands of criminals.

GLOSSARY

ammunition Projectiles, such as bullets, that are fired from a gun.

arsenal A collection or supply of weapons.

detonate To explode suddenly and violently, or to cause to explode.

evacuate To withdraw or remove (people or things) from an area, especially for reasons of safety.

harass To annoy or torment constantly or persistently.

homicide The killing of a human being by another.

hostile Extremely unfriendly or combative.

lenient Characterized by tolerance and lack of strictness, especially when administering punishment.

massacre The cruel and unnecessary killing of a number of people.

persecute To harass or oppress.

pipe bomb A small explosive device contained in a metal pipe, often homemade.

prohibit To forbid.

psychopathy A mental disorder marked especially by antisocial behavior.

sawed-off shotgun A shotgun with a shorter barrel than a regular shotgun. Sawing off the barrel makes the weapon easier to conceal.

sharpshooter Generally, a shooter known for accurate aim. In the military, it is a grade of proficiency above marksman and below expert in use of rifles and other weapons.

subculture A subgroup within a society that has a distinctive pattern of behaviors or attitudes.

Brady Center to Prevent Gun Violence
1225 Eye Street NW, Suite 1100
Washington, DC 20005
(202) 898-0792
Web site: http://www.bradycenter.org
The Brady Center is the largest nonpartisan, grassroots organization to prevent gun violence. The Brady Center works to educate the public about gun violence. It also works to enforce regulations to reduce gun violence by attempting to regulate the gun industry.

Canadian Safe School Network
111 Peter Street, Suite 409
Toronto, ON M5V 2H1
Canada
(416) 977-1050
Web site: http://www.canadiansafeschools.com
CSSN is a national, charitable organization dedicated to reducing youth violence and making schools and communities safer.

Center for the Prevention of School Violence
North Carolina Department of Juvenile Justice and
        Delinquency Prevention
4112 Pleasant Valley Road, Suite 214
Raleigh, NC 27612
(800) 299-6054
Web site: http://www.ncdjjdp.org/cpsv
One of the nation's first state school safety centers, the CPSV serves as a resource center and think tank for efforts that promote safer schools and foster positive youth development.

Coalition to Stop Gun Violence/Educational Fund to
    Stop Gun Violence
1023 15th Street NW, Suite 301
Washington, DC 20005
(202) 408-0061
E-mail: webmaster@csgv.org
Web site: http://www.csgv.org
A coalition comprised of forty-five national organizations working to reduce
gun violence, the CSGV includes religious organizations, child welfare
advocates, public health professionals, and social justice organizations.

The Institute on Violence and Destructive Behavior
1265 University of Oregon
Eugene, OR 97403-1265
(541) 346-5391
E-mail: ivdb@uoregon.edu
Web site: http://darkwing.uoregon.edu/ ~ivdb
The mission of the IVDB is to empower schools and social service agencies
to address violence and destructive behavior, at the point of school entry and
beyond, in order to ensure safety and to facilitate the academic achievement
and healthy social development of children and youth.

National Crime Prevention Council (NCPC)
2345 Crystal Drive, Fifth Floor
Arlington, VA 22202
(202) 466-6272
Web site: http://www.ncpc.org

The NCPC's goal is to keep communities safe from crime. To that end, it produces literature and offers programs that teach crime prevention techniques.

National School Safety Center
141 Duesenberg Drive, Suite 11
Westlake Village, CA 91362
(805) 373-9977
Web site: http://www.schoolsafety.us
The NSSC helps educate people on violence in U.S. schools. It does this by making literature and videos available on topics such as school safety, bullies in the classroom, and school crime.

Safe and Drug-Free Schools Program
United States Department of Education
400 Maryland Avenue SW
Washington, DC 20202-6123
(202) 260-3954
Web site: http://www.ed.gov/offices/OESE/SDFS
A U.S. Department of Education program devoted to education policy that promotes safe and drug-free schools.

Youth Crime Watch of America
9200 South Dadeland Boulevard, Suite 417
Miami, FL 33156
(305) 670-2409
E-mail: ycwa@ycwa.org

Deadly School and Campus Violence

Web site: http://www.ycwa.org
YCWA brings youth of all backgrounds together to identify and correct problems unique to their schools and communities.

Web Sites

Due to the changing nature of Internet links, Rosen Publishing has developed an online list of Web sites related to the subject of this book. This site is updated regularly. Please use this link to access the list:

http://www.rosenlinks.com/vas/sacm

FOR FURTHER READING

Barbour, Scott, ed. *How Can School Violence Be Prevented?* Farmington Hills, MI: Greenhaven Press, 2005.

Brown, Brooks, and Rob Merritt. *No Easy Answers: The Truth Behind Death at Columbine High School.* New York, NY: Lantern Books, 2002.

Carls, Beth, and Amy Looper. *I Wish I Knew What to Do?! . . . On What to Say to Get Bullies to Leave You Alone.* Houston, TX: MindOH! Foundation, 2005.

Fox, Cybelle, et al. *Rampage: The Social Roots of School Shootings.* New York, NY: Basic Books, 2005.

Hunnicutt, Susan, ed. *School Shootings.* Farmington Hills, MI: Greenhaven Press, 2006.

Kaufman, Gershen, Lev Raphael, and Pamela Espeland. *Stick Up for Yourself: Every Kid's Guide to Personal Power & Positive Self-Esteem.* Minneapolis, MN: Free Spirit Publishing, 1999.

Meyer, Adam. *The Last Domino.* New York, NY: G. P. Putnam's Sons, 2005.

Picoult, Jodi. *Nineteen Minutes.* New York, NY: Atria Books, 2007.

Strasser, Todd. *Give the Boy a Gun.* New York, NY: Simon Pulse, 2002.

BIBLIOGRAPHY

Cullen, Dave. "The Depressive and the Psychopath: At Last We Know Why the Columbine Killers Did It." *Slate*, April 20, 2004. Retrieved October 1, 2007 (http://slate.com/id/2099203).

Fox, James Alan, and Jack Levin. *Extreme Killing: Understanding Serial and Mass Murder.* Thousand Oaks, CA: Sage Publications, 2005.

Hughes, Sandra, and Harry Smith. "Arizona Gunman Had Threatened School." CBS News, October 29, 2002. Retrieved October 1, 2007 (http://www.cbsnews.com/stories/2002/10/30/national/main527553.shtml).

Jones, Tamara, and Joshua Partlow. "Pa. Killer Had Prepared for 'Long Siege.'" *Washington Post*, October 4, 2006. Retrieved October 1, 2007 (http://www.washingtonpost.com/wp-dyn/content/article/2006/10/04/AR2006100400331.html).

Larkin, Ralph W. *Comprehending Columbine*. Philadelphia, PA: Temple University Press, 2007.

Lieberman, Joseph. *The Shooting Game: The Making of School Shooters.* Santa Ana, CA: Seven Locks Press, 2006.

Newman, Katherine S. *Rampage: The Social Roots of School Shootings*. New York, NY: Basic Books, 2004.

Pawlak, Debra. "Just Another Summer Day: The Bath School Disaster." *MediaDrome*, 2000. Retrieved October 1, 2007 (http://www.themediadrome.com/content/articles/history_articles/disaster_in_bath.htm).

Ramsland, Katherine. *Inside the Minds of Mass Murderers.* Westport, CT: Praeger Publishers, 2005.

Thomas, R. Murray. *Violence in America's Schools: Understanding, Prevention, and Responses.* Westport, CT: Praeger Publishers, 2006.

Trump, Kenneth S. *Classroom Killers? Hallway Hostages? How Schools Can Prevent and Manage School Crises*. Thousand Oaks, CA: Corwin Press, Inc., 2000.

Virginia Tech Review Panel. *Mass Shootings at Virginia Tech: Report of the Review Panel*. Presented to Governor Kaine, Commonwealth of Virginia, 2007.

Vossekuil, B., R. Fein, M. Reddy, R. Borum, and W. Modzeleski. *The Final Report and Findings of the Safe School Initiative: Implications for the Prevention of School Attacks in the United States*. U.S. Department of Education, Office of Elementary and Secondary Education, Safe and Drug-Free Schools Program, and U.S. Secret Service, National Threat Assessment Center. Washington, DC, 2002.

INDEX

About the Author

Corona Brezina has written over a dozen titles for Rosen Publishing. Several of her previous books have also focused on topics related to current events and issues facing young adults. She lives in Chicago.

Photo Credits

Cover (left) © Robert Sullivan/Getty Images; cover (right) © Win McNamee/ Getty Images; p. 4 Courtesy NBC/Zuma Press; p. 8 © John T. Barr/Liaison Agency/Getty Images; p. 10 © Joyce Naltchayan/AFP/Getty Images; p. 11 © Howard Ruffner/Time & Life Pictures/Getty Images; p. 14 © Kevin Moloney/ Getty Images; pp. 15, 25, 29, 39, 49 © AP Images; p. 18 © Zuma Archive; p. 20 © Jefferson County Sheriff's Office/Zuma Press; p. 23 © Ethel Wolovitz/The Image Works; p. 26 © Paul Carter/AFP/Getty Images; p. 31 © Les Stone/ Zuma Press; p. 35 © Mark Leffingwell/Getty Images; p. 42 © Mark Wilson/ Getty Images; p. 43 © Sean Gallup/Getty Images; p. 46 © Eugene H. Louie/ San Jose Mercury News/Newscom; p. 51 © Steve Kagan/Liaison Agency/ Getty Images; p. 52 © Sean Cayton/The Image Works.

Designer: Nelson Sá; **Editor:** Nicholas Croce
Photo Researcher: Amy Feinberg